TO GOD BE THE GLORY

TAREY D. MEEKS

Meek &HUMBLE PUBLISHING

McKinney, Texas

TO GOD BE THE GLORY

Copyright © 2016 by Tarey D Meeks
McKinney, Texas 75069

ISBN- 978-0-9978878-0-8

Cover Design by Moore Designs

Published in McKinney, Texas, by Meek & Humble Publishing.

Library of Congress Cataloging-in-Publication Data:

Meeks, Tarey, 1963-
To God be the Glory/ Tarey D. Meeks

Contents

Acknowledgements

I would like to thank the people who have made this book possible:

First I would like to thank God for the gifts that He has blessed me with. I thank Him for opening doors and placing the right people at the right time in my life. Without Him, I am nothing.

To my mother, Athelgra Neville Gabriel, who always believed in me, long before I had a clue. For always telling me "girl, you got to do something with that".

To my family, Ronnie Meeks Sr., Ronnie Meeks, Jr., Taronika Meeks-Robinson and Ryan Meeks, just for loving me unconditionally and giving me the space and time to allow God to do His transformation.

To Moore Designs, for the best book cover design ever. You truly captured my vision.

Thank you all!

Preface

TO GOD BE THE GLORY is a compilation of poems that depict the miraculous transformation that took place in my life. Each poem reflects an event, thought, or time in my life that was difficult for me. The only way I was able to express it was to put it in writing. The only way to get through it was to write about it. I believe now that every word that God allowed me to write, was His way of preparing me for a time such as this. As I read each poem to gather the material for this book, I began to cry. God was using my own words to encourage me and minister to me. Nobody but God would know what I would need and when I would need it. It was as if the words I had written years ago were for the time that I was reading it; now, in the present. In the lines of each poem, my truth was being revealed to me. I was able to see what was in the root of my mindset and what it was that was holding me back. Everything in my life that was not a part of God's will for my life was unveiled and I was literally able to leave every emotion, struggle, stronghold, hinderance, and negative word ever spoken over my life right on the pages of this book. I was able to say goodbye to rejection; goodbye to fear and goodbye to my insecurities. Today, I know that I have changed and I choose to honor

God by using this gift that He has given to me. Choosing to believe in Him and follow Him, was the best decision of my life.

 After reading this poetry, you will have a better understanding of who I was, where I've been and who I am today. You will know some "truths" about Tarey.

I pray that everyone that reads these pages will be encouraged to know that there is a God, that His one and only Son, Jesus, died for us and that believing in Him is the only way to the Father. I pray that this work invokes healing to someone's heart, hope to someone's future, and encouragement to someone's soul. I also pray that each and every one of you realize that you too can be transformed by God, if you surrender your all to Him. I am who I am today because I believe that Jesus loves me. He wants me to let YOU know that He loves you the same. If He did it for me He will do it for you!!
I Love You All!!

Tarey D Meeks

On the outside looking in   1996

How can you know what I'm going through

When you haven't been where I've been

How can you sit back and judge me

When you're on the outside looking in

One day you see me and my eyes are bright red

My hair's all amiss and I look like the walking dead

You say I'm on drugs and I'm on the wrong track

It's not a monkey I'm dealing with

It's my kids on my back

And the cleaning and the ironing and trying

To pay all these bills

I'm a single parent struggling; I have dreams to fulfill

I didn't ask for this life, it's just the hand I was dealt

Compared to these wounds, what's one little welt

On a child who's disobedient, disrespectful and rude

He needs to learn discipline because the real world is crude

But who am I to teach him and show him the way

Let you tell my story I'm getting high everyday

But the truth is I'm handling it in the way I know how

Let me be judged by one who is greater than thou

So the next time you see me and I'm looking a little thin

Just remember you're on the outside looking in

Attitude 1996

Attitude is a state of mind

Indicative of a mood

That extends from a being that's

Insecure and even a little bit rude

Attitude is a way of carrying one's self

It can be done in a positive manner

It can be a disguise; it can be discreet

Or written on a face like a banner

Attitude can be a gift and can even

Be considered a merit

Attitude is like your old fake fur

It's all in how you wear it

Absence makes the heart grow fonder 1998

Before you left we used to do things together

Like ride out to the park or rent a movie during rainy weather

We'd take the kids to see Disney or spend a quiet evening at home

We had some fun times, some good times

Now I'm doing these things alone

You ask me if I miss you and of course you know I do

But sometimes it hurts and makes me cry when I think of you

I wish I could go back to the time before you were gone

But I can't so I sit here in my world all alone

They say absence makes the heart grow fonder

I wonder what is meant by that

Does it mean that no matter how long it takes

I will never want to turn back

The hands of time which wait for no one

My life it has to go on

Or does it mean that I'll love you forever

No matter how long you're gone

They say absence makes the heart grow fonder

I'm beginning to understand

But no matter how hard I try to be strong

I keep reaching for a stronger hand

To massage my feet at the end of the work day

And rub my back when I'm stressed

To be my friend and encourage me to keep

Striving to do my best

And as I lean toward that stronger hand

I realize that what they say is true

Absence does make the heart grow fonder

But of someone other than you

My eyes wide shut 2000

It may be obvious to some
When he doesn't come home
Or return your 9-1-1 page
what's really going on
But I had my eyes wide shut

It may be obvious to some,
When family time is cut short
Or doesn't exist at all
what's really going on
But I had my eyes wide shut

It may be obvious to some
When his place at the dinner table
Is empty because he's working late…again
What's really going on
But I had my eyes wide shut

Sometimes it's hard to see
The forest for the trees

I blamed myself

And I was eager to please

Now I don't bother to page him

I don't wait up anymore

There once were five places at the table

Now there are four

I got caught up because of the love I feel

Always accepting the lie as real

But the truth has a way of coming to light

Now my eyes wide shut

Have been blessed with sight!

Word to a mother 2001

Because you've never seen her cry

You think she doesn't feel any pain

Because you can't find the answer

You just give her the blame

Do you really think she's capable of?

All the deceit you claim she's done

Or are you trying not to face the facts

About what happened to your son

He's a grown man who's responsible

For his own fate

Because he doesn't turn out the way you want

You blame it on his mate

That's the easy way out

Or at least that's the way it seems

Because you know that it haunts you

In each and every one of your dreams

All she did was love and cherish him

Any choices he made were his own

The way you treated her when it all went down

Was just ugly to the bone

Did you try to get to know her?

Or did you judge her at just one glance

I bet you already counted her out

Before she had a chance

They really really love each other with all their

Heart and soul

You can't keep them apart forever

And you'll slowly lose control

You know the tighter you try to pull those reigns

The further away he'll flee

You can't keep a man from his family if that's where he wants to be

So make it easier on yourself let him make up his own mind

He's paid the price for his past mistakes he won't get back in that bind

I know you want to protect him but in reality your job is done

Let him go to his wife to help her raise their kids

He'll prove to you he's a good son

Just Me 2009

In my attempts to come to grips with who I am, I sometimes get it twisted with who people think I am.

I want to be who I need to be for those who need me, but the complexities of my personality confuse them of my accessibility.

I am complete, but I feel there's something missing.

I am complacent but I'm constantly dismissing the accolades as a plan of the enemy to get me off guard, cause me to be weak.

And in my own eyes, I have lost the battle within.

Why must I give in to sin?

Why can't I be NOW who God wants me to be in the end?

I am competent, but at times I just don't understand Why me?

Why now?

Who am I that they want to befriend me?

Can't they see the inner me?

I love and I love hard, but sometimes it's hard to love.

I reach out but I'm not touched.

I listen but I'm not heard.

All it takes is just one smile, one look, one touch, one word.

I am to you, who you are to me.

If I'm nothing to you, then who should you be to me?

I'm easy, but don't push me.

I don't fight back, but I won't look back

But that's Just Me.

So Amazin' 6/2/13

Lord you're so amazin'

You show yourself to me

Day out and day in

I can look back and see

How you were always there for me

Even when I thought I was alone

You were the only one

With your still quiet voice

That kept me sane

Kept me from committing the unthinkable

Act of violence

Upon myself or someone else

 You kept me stable

When I was unable

Kept me from jumping over the ledge

When I was on the edge

Of blackness

In the middle of my madness

Your voice brought me

Back to life back to reality

You pointed me toward my destiny

It is a hard battle

I must confess

Dueling with my tainted flesh

Because the enemy don't fight fair

He kept hitting me from everywhere

He was kickin' up my past

Trynna make sure my present didn't last

He Tried to do a sneak attack

On my future

To keep my dreams in capture

He couldn't take a risk on my rapture

'Cause I was going somewhere

Jesus already paid the fare

When he transformed my mind

It's like time did a rewind

I wasn't who I was but who he said I'd be

Some had to do a double take

To make sure it was me

Standing so beautifully and wonderfully made

Some haters were dismayed

They thought I was down for the count

Didn't think that I would amount

To one thin dime

But Jesus is always on time

He never counted me out or

Marked me for dead

Instead his hand of blessing was upon my head

He said follow me child let me lead the way

He already knew the makings of this day

I praise Him, I thank Him, I lift Him

Up I Glorify His Name

I shout it from the mountain top

I show no shame

Oh if it had not been for the Lord on my side

I woulda died, lost in my pride

My world turned up side

Down the wrong path

You do the math

Jesus knew me before I was born

He predestined my life

From each and every victory

Down to every little strife

Yes He has the final say

And His word is unchangin'

Yes Lord You're so Amazin'

Love never fails 6/17/13

He started picking fights

Almost every other night

He didn't eat my home cooked meals

Because he didn't have an appetite

He started coming in late

Then staying out all night

I guess it was safe to say

My marriage wasn't alright

I'd ask what's going on

 Are you seeing someone else?

Has our love grown cold

Like those cases on the shelf

But the FBI nor CSI

Could put together the clues

To solve this horrible crime

Taking place in my house of blues

I'm feeling abused and misused

But I refuse

To let it get the best of me

Because I've got people to see

So I pick up the mask

The one that best suits my task

And I walk like it don't matter

I talk, but it's only chitter chatter

Because I'm really numb and

You can't imagine what I have to

Succumb

To

Don't know if I'm coming or going

But on my face I'm not showin

The hurt, the pain

The betrayal and who's to blame

Lord I've prayed, I've cried

I've fasted, I've tried

I can't hold on any longer

Why can't this black woman

Be stronger

It seemed the closer I drew to God

The farther apart we became

That was our life on the inside

But on the outside we still played the game

Because the truth would bring shame

The truth would reveal the lie

In order to bring this marriage back to life

Something had to die

So I let go

 of the charade

And reached to the Lord above

To renew my mind and touch my heart

So that I could continue to love

And be patient and kind

You must think I'm outta my mind

To stick with,

 to deal with,

 put up with this mess

Who does he think I am, I don't have an S on my chest

But with God all things are possible

And things aren't always what they seem

Only God knows the heart of a man

Only God knows what it all means

So I surrender my life and my will to the Lord

His Word is all that prevails

Therefore what God has joined together with love

Never fails

Who is She 6/18/13

She is a woman

Made from the rib of a man

One man

Her man

Made from the part that protects

His heart

Put together by God

Until death brings them apart

Of each other the two become one

The bond that can't come undone

By anyone under the sun

When you realize what you're destined for

You stand for more

Than the average Joe

They think they all know

What they woulda, coulda, shoulda done

When she was the only one

Going through, Crying through, Praying through

She got her answers too

From God and Him alone

Don't matter what behaviors

You wouldn't condone

She knew her creator

Because he created her

To be who she was

To stand strong through the trials

To stand strong through the pains

So hard it made her back bend

But she knew in the end

They both would win

Because it was in God's plan

To use her to bring a man

One man, Her man

To his rightful place by the throne

And turn their house into a home

And her children will rise and

Call her blessed

And know why she went through

All that mess

That had her stressed

And she couldn't rest

'til she put her trust in God

And let Him lead the way

To the life He had already planned for them

To the ministry that was planted within

He'd say she was virtuous

And more precious than a ruby

I'd say thank you God that

She is Me!

Beauty for Ashes 3/25/14

Beauty is in the eye of the beholder

But as I look in to the mirror at my life before me

I turn in shame

There is no beauty in me

That I see

I feel no matter what I do

I can't erase, I can't escape

My weaknesses, my shortcomings

My insecurities

I'm always falling

One step shorter

Than those around me

So I put a cloak over the mirror

In hopes my perception is clearer

But the blackness

Only adds to my madness

And I can't get a grip on my sadness

Because

I'm staring at a blank canvas

My heart

The part that is the soul of me

The part of me that deceives me because it is wicked

I can't even trust it

So I wax it cold

And I stand tall and bold

So you can't see through me

You can't see the real me

The little girl who let mommy down

Crying so many tears

I thought I would drown

In them, Because I can't swim

In this sea of guilt, rejection,

Denial, disgrace

I'm pulling at hairs

And yet

not one's out of place

I'm careful not to leave a trace

Of the secret place

My mind wanders or

My thoughts ponder

Sometimes I write them down

And lock it up with a key

Those sacred pages shall no other eyes see

I pray dear Lord how could this be

That this tainted face I see is me

Beauty is in the eye of the beholder

The One who knew me before I was born

Knew me before I was formed

In my mother's womb

He already knew my agony of doom

He knew I was broken

Feeling damaged and insignificant

Then He chose me and molded me

And called it magnificent

You see I was ready to call it quits

Throw in the towel

And chalk it up as a loss

But he reminded me that

The battle was won

Cause He already paid the cost

He said remove the cloak of failures

Of heaviness and dismays

And prepare to receive the

Garment of Praise

Because I have gone ahead

And fought against the masses

Turning your adversities into ashes

Before the thunder claps and the lightning flashes

You have become who I have created you to be

And now you are blessed

To behold your own beauty

The Other Woman 8/21/14

He loves me

He loves me not

Or maybe he forgot

That we tied the knot

Together **X** amount of years

Can't understand **Y** I've shed so many tears

Of pain and not joy

Playing with my heart

Like a boy with a brand new toy

I don't pretend to understand

How it all got out of hand

I just know that this isn't

What God planned

He loves me

He loves me not

Or maybe it's just a plot

Him thinking there's something better

Than what he's got

Seeking and searching but never finding

A love that was binding

Only going in circles, spinning and winding

Like a dog chasing its tail

Not able to see

Because of the veil

Of deceit over his eyes

So confused he believes the lies

That the world he lives on the outside

Can somehow become the bright side

Of a situation he's not ready to face

That's why he's running the race

To please the folk

Who don't mean him no good

He'd rather be down with the hood

Than do what he knows he should

And he can't hear my voice

In the middle of the night

Pleading and praying

That he turns to the light

It seems that I have become the enemy

And to turn away from me

Is the remedy

To the pain he feels inside

He'll never let us know the tears he's cried

Too filled up with pride

Done slipped and got his nose opened wide

By the chick on the side

No longer laying his head on my bosom

Because I have become

 the other woman

He loves me

He loves me not

My Sister 8/24/14

I met her in the sanctuary

Oh Mary Mary quite contrary

She wanted to know

Just what made my garden grow

So she took my hand and

Came along for the ride

Her only intent

Was to get on the inside

Of my C230

She rode in it with style

Brought it back on empty

With nothing but a smile

And that's ok

Cause I had it like that

Big daddy is always waiting

To hand lil mama a stack

Yeah I saw that twinkle in her eye

A look I couldn't deny

I didn't want to believe it

My mind couldn't conceive it

That she was eager to receive it

That she was willing to put

The knife in my back

To get my honey in the sack

Because she thought my grass was greener

I wish I coulda seen her

When it was all said and done

After she thought she would be the one

That was gonna take my place

I wanted to laugh but it was a disgrace

When he was riding off with yet another

And leaving her staring into space

Now she has what I have, And she felt what I felt

Her heart broken into pieces

And him

Another notch on his belt

But I pray for my sister

That God heals her pain

That he removes what has tainted her

So she won't do that again

That she learns to love herself

As I am learning to do

God has renewed my mind

And changed my heart

So that on this day my sister, I can say

I Forgive You!

To Be 8/28/14

Dark Skinned, light skinned

Why does it matter

What color skin I'm wrapped in

True beauty comes from within

The heart and soul of a being

The words that come out of their mouths

Not the amount of melanin you're seeing

But what does it mean

To your young daughter

The only piece of chocolate

In the middle of the creamy colored skin

Of her kin

Feeling like a pig brought out to slaughter

Only to be picked over

Then left in the pen

Not to be chosen

She thinks

Because of her skin

Or maybe it's the texture of her hair

Or the fact that not much is there

It's not soft, it's not curly

Like theirs

She doesn't get

"Oh look, how pretty"

Just stares

No special hugs or kisses

Only nonchalant dismisses

Feeling of just being tolerated

Because of family ties

Feeling less than the others

No matter how hard she tries

To fit in

Doing things just because

Everybody else was

Her heart no way in it

Always trailing at the end

Of the line

Walking way behind

The crew

Feeling a struggle in her spirit

But she never knew

There was a calling on her life

That didn't allow her to get lost

But to hold her head high

And count up the cost

To be different

To be set apart

To acknowledge that her beauty

Was in her heart

That her very being was a plan

Right from the start

Before she was created

In her mother's womb

Her story was foretold

Predestined by the one from whom

All blessings flow

Lord now I know

Those things you allowed

Were only to make me grow

Into the woman I have become

So fearfully and wonderfully made by you

Cared for by you

Loved by you

Nothing else will matter

Only my days of latter

Are brighter

Are greater

I give all praises to the creator

For releasing the little girl in me

Bound up with bitterness

And insecurities

Allowing the woman inside of me

To be set free

From herself

And the issues that I hid

About to cause a meltdown

God forbid

The joy of the Lord is my strength

And the time on my knees

Was time well spent

Much more valuable

Because my God is infallible

More power than X to the third

Able to transform me

With just one little word

BE

And I am

Who He says I am

Able to defeat the enemy

In a single bound

Didn't matter if my skin

Was light or dark brown

Long hair don't care

To nobody but Samson

My God you're the only one

I can lean and depend on

I WILL lean and depend on

And when I get to the place

Where I can look at my face

And see my beauty

As you created it

Then I will know it was

All worth it

To allow God to birth it

Out of me

The power to reach another

Young girl or mother

With just a single word

BE!

Case Closed 09/16/14

Sometimes I get a glimpse

Or what some may call a look-see

Of an **SVU** crime scene

And the victim is me

No clear faces

Just body parts in places

That they shouldn't be

I pray that I'm dreaming

Then I realize I'm awake

To imagine that I was violated

Is a nightmare I can't shake

I don't know when

Or who or why

But this haunting in my spirit

Is a feeling I can't deny

No tell-tale bruises to build my case

Just flashback moments

That I can't erase

And the unsub has disappeared

WITHOUT A TRACE

So I kept my own secret

For to tell would be my disgrace

I keep it all bottled in

Shoved deep down into a space

That's unreachable by normal measures

Embedded deep in crevices

Only released when I'm under the pressures

Of day to day life

I'm flying off the handle

Trying to uncover the **SCANDAL**

That takes place in my mind

Or is it reality

The visions are so plain

And some nights I can't sleep

When I hear the footsteps creep

Down the long dark pathway

Of my memory

My sensory

Vision must be impaired

My future beware

Because I'm fully prepared

Ready or not

Like a thickening plot

Full of **CRIMINAL MINDS**

And **MAJOR CRIMES**

It's funny how I'm the one doing the time

A prisoner to my own mind

They're all lucky I haven't **SNAPPED**

Being trapped

By the **law with no order**

Now it's way past the **48TH HOUR**

But to the one who has the power

Doesn't matter how long the

Situations been dead

"talitha cumi, arise from your bed"

And then there was life

From the words that He said

No need for the chalk line

No need for the yellow tape

The evidence has been made clear

And the enemy can't escape

It was only a setback for a setup

So if you missed a step

You better hurry and catch up

You know time waits for no one

And the end is near

But there's nothing to fear

If you fear nothing

Case Closed

Unchangeable 4/2/15

My life has been like

A merry go round

Things spinning out

Of control

Going back and forth

Up and down

More entertaining than

A circus clown

One minute I'm here

The next one I'm there

One day I'm smiling

And in the next moment

Only a blank stare

Not focused on anything

The spinning has got me dizzy

I'm constantly moving

To keep busy

Doing nothing

going no where

Because my focus

Is out of sync

I don't have time to

Worry about what "they" think

Because my ship's about to sink

Too much weight on me

Carrying issues I shouldn't be

Walking around feeling

Like a misfit

But in reality

No one's paying me any mind

Not one bit

In love today

Out of love tomorrow

A heart full of sorrow

For myself

The guilt and the shame

I have no one to blame

For the confusion

Hitting me so hard

I'm diagnosed with a contusion

My left nor my right brain

Has a function

I'm feeling trapped

In this junction

Like the little engine

That could

I think I can, I think I can

I think I can

Fight this uphill battle

I'm running aimlessly

Like cattle

Out to slaughter

Then I realize

I'm somebody's daughter

Who says with a price

I bought her

Yes I have a father

Jesus, who holds me in

His arms

As my mind goes in circles

He has a strong steady hand

That calms seas and does miracles

When my thoughts

Are juggling

And in my faith walk

I'm struggling

My day to day schedule

Is demanding

He gives me a peace that

Surpasses all understanding

Or when the storm causes the waves

To rise against me

To rock me and break me

And knock against my

Strong exterior

Like the enemy whispering in my ear

That I am inferior

Coming only to steal, destroy and kill

But my Father commands

Peace be still

And all is well

And I love Him because He first

Loved me

There's nothing that I can do to be

Set free

Of his unconditional love

The only constant in my life

Even when I wasn't aware

That He was there

He promised He would never

Leave me nor forsake me

I'm the one with the doubt

And unbelief

It don't matter that at times

I am unable, unstable, or incapable

My Father remains the same

He's UNCHANGEABLE.

Dear Father 5/1/15

Father forgive me when I wonder
How far you're going to bring me
How much longer must I go through
To be who you called me to be

I know you didn't bring me this far to leave me
The enemy whispering in my ear
To deceive me
That
I walked away from what I know
My safe comfort zone
To a place hundreds of miles away
Now I'm all alone

It seemed the moment I took your hand
My life began to fall apart
When in fact the moment I surrendered
You gave me a brand new start

You brought me out to show me

Exactly who You are

To lift me from a low dark place

And show me that I am a star

Ignoring the doubts of the naysayers

"she won't make it" "yeah, I know she'll be back"

I grab tighter to Your hand and hold on to Your Word

Knowing in You there is nothing that I will lack

Father forgive me when I get weak

And want to retreat

To avoid some possible shame

Because quickly I remember

That my journey

Is only

to bring Glory to Your name.

Ready for Battle 5/3/14

I've been told by many

That I'm strong.

That I handle my challenges gracefully

But they're wrong

What they see on the outside

Is a façade

Because I'm impeccably dressed

In my camouflage

The gear that's typically

Used for war

So the fiery darts bounce off

And don't leave a scar

From top to bottom

From head to toe

They only see what I want

Them to know

Because I've mastered the masquerade

Of make believe and pretend

My mind set every morning

Was "Let the games begin"

So when I roll out of bed in

The morning

To get on my way

I pick out the wardrobe

That suits my role for the day

Thinking that if I wore the

Dress and shoes with the matching clutch

The fact that I was

Broken and bitter

Wouldn't matter so much

Or the Brazilian weave

Hanging down to my behind

Would somehow conceal the

Crazy thoughts in my mind

You see

I was trying so hard to

Cover up

What God was trying to reveal to me

What would be the key

To set me free

From the bondage I was in

A slave to sin

To recognize that He positioned

Me in a fight

That I was predestined to win

That no matter what I come against

In each and every day

He'll give me just enough light

For the step I'm on

Then

He will lead the way

No more remy, dreamweaver or

Brazilian for affirmation

I now adorn my head

With the helmet of salvation

Not worried about a broken heart

Due to the lack of another's kindness

Because now I'm fully protected

With my breastplate of righteousness

Not concerned with a waist trainer

That slims me down to the size of my youth

Instead I trust the Lord and girt my loins

With the belt of truth

Now I never wore stilettos or

Louboutins on my feet

But now they're laced

As I face the enemy

With the preparation of the gospel of peace

As I grab the sword of the spirit

And the shield of faith

My ensemble is complete

I'm dressed in the full armour of God

I'm ready to defeat

The enemy

That I recognize is

Not my brother, my sister or my friend

But the spirit forces of wickedness

They never give up

They keep fighting up to the end

But no longer am I weighed down

With issues that made me fragile

That was then

This is now

Today,

I'm ready for battle!!

Who's Right 5/23/15

When I was 18 years' old

I was thinking

That means I'm grown

But the things I know now

Back then I wish I could

Have known

That the decisions I made with

No wisdom to back it

Would cause a domino effect

and I couldn't re-stack it

No matter how hard I tried

You can't undo a procedure

That leaves your womb

Full of scars

And your mind with thoughts

Of wars

Between right and wrong

But who's right and who's wrong

because it's my body

Was it my choice?

My seed didn't have a chance

Because she didn't

Have a voice

I didn't hear her then

But I hear her now

Crying and saying

Why mommy? How?

Could you do such a thing

And not take the time to consider

The joy I might bring

To what seemed like a

Dreadful situation

And was I not

God's creation

Father forgive me

For playing your role

For the life I stole

That was a part of me

That I was ashamed that

The world would see

And cause me to feel

Less than I already be

Feeling

This pain that could be the very death of me

Father forgive me

I'm a murderer

Too afraid I wouldn't know

How to nurture her

So I took the easy way out

Or so I thought

But what I brought

Was something for the enemy

To hold over my head

Where I'd feel condemned

Instead

Of knowing that the Father

Would give me freedom

From the sins of my past

And my broken heartedness

Wouldn't last

And that He loves me

To transform me

And give me a new heart

With wisdom not to abort

The plans He has for my life

To stay on the path

Towards the light

And with a clear understanding

Of who's right!

Let it go 5/26/15

How is it that I love you

So much lord

But still it seems I don't get it

How is it that

When there's a move of God

Sometimes I just miss it

I read and pray your word

Each day

Without it

My day couldn't start

So why is it that

 I continue to hold

So much anger & bitterness

In my heart

My Lord you know how

Much I pray for

These strongholds to let me be

That they release the hold they

Have on me

So I can be set free

I thought I had forgiven

All those I needed to forgive

But somehow these ungodly

Issues continue to live

A strong hold is defined

As a place of survival

Or a place of refuge

So I can deduce and conclude

That it is

Something that **I** refuse

To let go of

Stronghold

Strong hold

Yes I

Have a stronghold

It doesn't have me

I

Have to let **IT** go

To be set free

But in this moment I can

Hide behind it

Because I really don't want to be seen

It's all I know

I don't want to let go

But I have to

If I want God to clean

My heart

And renew my mind

Giving me the strength

To leave those struggles behind

to take the authority

That was given to me

And take control of this flesh

And declare and decree

That as of this day

I'm truly done with this mess

I can choose not to be angry or bitter

And let the enemy have his way

But allow the spirit of God

To rule and abide

In me this very day

Now I can freely

Surrender to the Lord

And allow my spirit to grow

Knowing that finally

I

Have let it go!

Are you Ready? 7/26/15

Are you Ready?

You say you want more

I say

Be careful of what you're

Asking for

His glory is too much to contain

It's impossible to catch a glimpse

yet still remain the same

You gotta be ready for change

Are you Ready?

To take it to the next level

You see

Every challenge ain't always

A trick of the devil

If you are to share in God's glory

You have to share in His suf-fer-ring

And stop all this shuf-ful-ing

Between religion and traditions

Heresies and seditions

And get into position

To receive   by faith

It's the only way to please Him

Fall down to your knees then

Thank Him

Are You Ready?

Ask and He'll give

Seek and you'll find

He doesn't want one soul

Left behind

But before He makes you

He has to break you

And take you

Through the valley

Of the shadow of death

Grasping for your last breath

Going through trials and tribulations

Denials and revelations

Countless tears ever flowing

And you don't even know

If you're coming or going

Are You Ready?

For your crooked road

To be made straight

That will lead you

To the heavenly gate

Where you meet your fate

Count your blessings

One by one

That you hear well done

That your race was well run

Because you didn't faint or

Get weary

Some naysayers are looking leery

But the truth is in His Word

And God never lies

His wonderfulness can't be denied

He's been tested and tried

But His faithfulness still abides

So I admonish you

To continue to press

For it is written

"every knee shall bow and

EVERY tongue shall confess"

Are You Ready??

Mirror Mirror 8/16/15

Mirror Mirror on the wall

Who's the fairest of them all

You reflect what I place before you

But God sees it all

I can pretend before man

With the mask that I wear

And shout with my hands up

Like I just don't care

But who wants to go through the motions

And end up where they began

All bruised up and out of breath

And you never even   ran

The race

Down the path

That God placed before you

Too busy in denial

Still trapped in what   you   knew

And not taking heed to the

Voice of God

That becomes evident in

Many ways

But you're not phased

Or amazed

Because the messenger's

Not who you thought

Shoulda brought

You the word

Mirror Mirror on the wall

Who's the fairest of them all

Will you catch me before I fall

It's time to be who God

Called me to be

But if I remove my mask

Will I like what I see

I can keep on pretending

And get left behind

Or step out in faith

With a renewed mind

Where my praise comes from my heart

And I move when God says move

And I prove

That I trust and believe Him

Mirror Mirror on the wall

Am I the fairest of them all

Tomorrow 9/13/15

Thinking of lost moments and wasted time

And

Taking chances on things that don't matter

Broken vows and broken hearts

Causing stable minds to scatter

Letting the enemy take the upper hand

While you're thinking you're in command

Like a rebel without a cause

Who's perpetrating to get an applause

In your mind you've got it made

When all of your followers

Are really throwing shade

It doesn't make sense to play make believe

Because

They're gonna tweet it

The way they perceive it

And once you send it

Oops

You can't delete it

So much role playing

Now you're the one confused

But

What does it gain you to win the world

When you have your soul to lose

It's time for you to choose

Life or death

It's

Black or white

No in between

No lukewarm

But

Be ye transformed

By the renewing of your mind

While you still have time

Because

Things will begin to pass you by

And

Slip out of your hands

And

what you thought you had

Will become

The prize of the next man

You better get with God's plan

You see

Nothing good is promised to the sinner

There are no guarantees

That Only comes in repentance

After falling on your knees

Saying Father forgive me

For my treacherous deeds

Thinking you could do what you want

Thinking you could do what you please

Setting yourself up for demise

Walking around with blinded eyes

Hurting those you claim to love

What were you thinking of?

But it's not too late

To right the wrong

God will give your heart

A brand new song

Surrender this day

Your life and will to the Son

Don't wait until tomorrow

Because

Tomorrow may never come!!

No greater love 11/26/15

As I looked through my window

At the rising sun in the sky

I remember

That the reason I'm able to do so

Is because

Somebody had to die

Every breath that I take

To keep me going another day

Is possible

Because the LAST one He took

Made the way

Every lash on His back

Cut deep into His skin

But

He endured it

So we wouldn't have to live in sin

The nails that they bore

Into His hands and feet

Are evidence that

We don't have to live in defeat

Everything we could possibly be guilty of

He carried it to the cross

And yet

We still deny Him and follow the lost

He paid it all

We have so much to be thankful for

But we got it all twisted

Some have died and missed it

And others made a cross with

Their fingers and kissed it

Taking lightly the sacrifice that was made

Not fully acknowledging

The price that was paid

He knew what we would face

That it would be

More than we could bare

So he went and prepared a place

Yet we act like we don't care

We turn our backs, we disobey

His commandments

We just don't keep

But when we lay at night

We're confident

That we will rise up from our sleep

Like we're entitled to this life we live

And it isn't even our own

Our very existence

Is because of

The unconditional love He's shown

The word says forgive

But that's a problem for us

If we count up our transgressions

The time keeper would bust

On but trust

He

Is faithful and just

To forgive the unthinkable things we've done

Every single one

You see

Every part of His agenda is about us

How much of ours is about Him

His sacrifice for us was intentional

Not just a silly whim

But we have so many excuses

To justify our behavior

Instead of following the example

Demonstrated by our savior

considering that all He's done

We're unworthy of

Brings me to the conclusion

There is no greater love